Rough

BOOKS BY DEBORAH DIGGES

POEMS

Rough Music   1995
Late in the Millennium   1989
Vesper Sparrows   1986

A MEMOIR

Fugitive Spring   1991

Rough Music

DEBORAH DIGGES

ALFRED A KNOPF

NEW YORK   1996

THIS IS A BORZOI BOOK
PUBLISHED BY ALFRED A. KNOPF, INC.

Grateful acknowledgement is made to the following magazines in which the poems in this book appeared, some in slightly different versions:

American Poetry Review: "Akhmatova."

Antaeus: "Rune for the Parable of Despair," "Tombs of the Muses," "Blue Willow," "In-House Harvest," "London Zoo."

The Atlantic Monthly: "The Little Book of Hand Shadows."

The New Yorker: "For the Lost Adolescent," "Nursing the Hamster," "Morning After a Blizzard," "Broom."

The New York Times: "Apples."

Ploughshares: "My Amaryllis," "Chekhov's Darling" (under the title "The Afterlife.")

Provincetown Arts: "Rough Music," "The Story of the Lighthouse."

Yale Review: "Late Summer."

"My Amaryllis" appeared in *Best American Poetry*, Charles Scribners Publishers, 1992. "Rough Music" won a Pushcart Prize in 1993. "Rock, Scissors, Paper" originally appeared in *New American Poets of the 90's*, edited by Jack Myers and Roger Weingarten, © 1991 by Jack Myers and Roger Weingarten, and is reprinted here courtesy of David R. Godine, Publisher, Inc.

The first epigraph is taken from a letter by John Keats to his brother, the second from Randall Jarrell's poem, "Seele im Raum," the third from a Jacobite hymn, and the last from Anna Akhmatova's "Requiem."

Grateful acknowledgment is made to Farrar, Straus & Giroux, Inc., and to Faber and Faber Limited for permission to reprint an excerpt from *"Seele im Raum"* from *The Complete Poems* by Randall Jarrell, © 1969 by Mrs. Randall Jarrell. Rights in the United Kingdom administered by Faber and Faber Limited, London. Reprinted by permission of Farrar, Straus & Giroux, Inc., and Faber and Faber Limited.

Library of Congress Cataloging-in-Publication Data

Digges, Deborah.
    Rough music: poems/by Deborah Digges.—1st ed.
        p.   cm.
    ISBN 0-679-44176-X
    I. Title.
PS3554.I3922R68   1995   95-15834
811'.54—dc20   CIP

Manufactured in the United States of America
Published September 23, 1995
Second Printing, August 1996

For Stephen *and* Charles,
for Trevor, *and* Susan, *and* Robin, *and* Gerry,
and Max, *and for* Frank.

Many doors are set open, but all dark—
We are in a mist.

Shall I make sense or shall I tell the truth?
Choose either—I cannot do both.

Now all is done that can be done
and all is done in vain.

Nevermind, I was not unprepared.

Contents

Rough Music

Broom

More than my sixteen rented houses and their eighty or so rooms
held up by stone or cinderblock foundations,
most facing north, with useless basements,
wrought iron fences to the curb,
beat-up black mailboxes—
eagles impaled through breasts to edifice—
or set like lighthouses
some distance from the stoop a thousand miles inland,

or close enough to sea the sea gulls
settled mornings in the playing fields I passed
on this continent and others
as I walked my sons to school or to the train—

more than the kitchen door frames where is carved the progress
of their growth, one then the other on his birthday
backed against a wall, almost on tiptoe—

and more than the ruler
I have laid across their skulls
where the older's brown hair like my own,
or the younger's blond like his father's, covered abundantly
what was once only a swatch of scalp
I'd touch as they slept to know their hearts beat—

more than the height at which, and in this house,
the markings stopped like stairs leading to ground level,
and they walked out into the world,
dogged, no doubt, by the ghost of the man, their father,
and the men who tried to be their fathers,
father their wildness—

and more, even, than the high sashed windows
and windows sliding sideways
through which I watched for them, sometimes squinting,
sometimes through my hands cupped on cold glass

3

trying to see in the dark my men approaching,
my breath blinding me,
the first born surely the man I would have married,
the second, me in his man's body—

more than the locks left open and the creaking steps,
the books left open like mirrors on the floor
and the sinks where we washed our faces
and the beds above which our threefold dreams collided,

I have loved the broom I took into my hands
and crossed the threshold to begin again,
whose straw I wore to nothing,
whose shaft I could use to straighten a tree, or break
across my knee to kindle the first winter fire,
or use to stir the fire,

broom whose stave is pine or hickory,
and whose skirt of birch-spray and heather
offers itself up as nest matter,
arcs like the equator
in the corner, could we see far enough,
or is parted one way like my hair.

Once I asked myself, when was I happy?
I was looking at a February sky.
When did the light hold me and I didn't struggle?
And it came to me, an image
of myself in a doorway, a broom in my hand,
sweeping out beach sand, salt, soot,
pollen and pine needles, the last December leaves,
and mud wasps, moths, flies crushed to wafers,
and spring's first seed husks,
and then the final tufts like down, and red bud petals
like autumn leaves— so many petals—

sweeping out the soil the boys tracked in
from burying in the new yard another animal—

4

broom leaving in tact the spiders' webs,
careful of those,
and careful when I danced with the broom,
that no one was watching,
and when I hacked at the floor
with the broom like an axe, jammed handle through glass
as if the house were burning and I must abandon ship
as I wept over a man's faithlessness, or wept over my own—

and so the broom became
an oar that parted waters, raft-keel and mast, or twirled
around and around on the back lawn,
a sort of compass through whose blurred counter-motion
the woods became a gathering of brooms,
onlooking or ancestral.

I thought I could grow old here,
safe among the ghosts, each welcomed,
yes, welcomed back for once, into this house, these rooms

in which I have got down on hands and knees and swept my hair
across my two sons' broad tan backs,
and swept my hair across you, swinging my head,
lost in the motion,
lost swaying up and down the whole length of your body,
my hair tangling in your hair,
our hair matted with sweat and my own cum, and semen,
lost swaying, smelling you,
smelling you humming,
gone in the motion, back and forth, sweeping.

Late Summer

The wild late summer gardens
refuse to be led in chorus, and the sparrows,
those minor saints.
Even Therese, *little flower of Jesus,*
will not answer to her name,
but gathers in her feathers anthills of dust like holy water,
as in a former life she gathered up her lice-infested skirts,
and wading into the Seine,
leveed a branch against the currents,
fished out the sacks full of drowned litters.
Now she carries the river with her in her drab brown wings,
carries the very codings of the weeds
in which she knelt,
and with a sugar spoon turned over the soil
for each small grave,
and lined the fledglings' holes with milkweed,
and laid the virus running through the earth.
There are those who save only the picture of the child smiling,
the summer tree.
Love doesn't change us.
Love remains the thing resisted,
a sky-colored glass the trapped bird bloodies.
Maybe Therese, following her calling,
wished the mockingbird silence in the convent orchards,
and all the warblers locked inside its song.
Maybe she dreamed her hands floating her own sputum-stained, bile-
stinking pillow over
her coughing sisters' faces, cell by cell,
as she sang to them in tongues, blood tongues and bone
and the many stone tongues of her sex,
her voice a buzz above their struggling like bees
drowning in honey,
sang them under what she herself so longed for,
weight of the earth, a baptismal dark.
Mercy's at best approximate,
like the first weeks of blindness

before the other senses' stunned quartet have learned to translate
inside the skull's black paradise
some recovery of touch, this odor of apples, sea-wind,
hearth-fire, this prophecy
of rain or danger,
this autumn or spring dryness in the leaves.

Tombs of the Muses

Fucking up the world's the least of it—
I'd say they're fourteen or fifteen
who take their time preparing the underpass's south wall,
the whole a mildew-black rotunda
seeping the spray of a million tires.
From the harbor drifts in fish-stink that bleeds green
from the dome, and a protein smell like old books,
and the smell of the river thawing.
Beyond us Boston's abandoned train cars junk the sunrise,
all the windows dark tongues spilling asbestos,
the space inside so noxious
even the cops steer clear, even the dealers.
But not the boys,
enough of the child in their truant voices I could weep—
the way you see them sometimes
scaling a playground's chain-links—
enough of the man I keep a distance.
They're mixing something like a fresco plaster,
sand, some kitchen flour into a latex base they stole,
they brag to me, from a church basement.
Now over the obscenities, over the characters
of wild dogs, gangsters, over the names,
a thousand signatures, at least—
over my own son's maybe—
they balance on a car door riding rat-chewed coach seats,
they roller-spread a sky.
One of them walks it off ten feet, ten paces,
as the shaman must have at a sacred cave's entrance.
So they begin their elegy for a friend dead of an overdose.
I ask of what.
One throws a bottle at the wall.
They laugh, *man, everything* . . .
Through the rush hour traffic like the gods roaring above us
and the dice throws of commuters thinning on the Pike,
such a thing takes shape by their own hands,
spray-painted, many colored.

8

An epitaph of sweeps and angles builds a face
whose blue-black rasta braided hair's bandanaed,
so many earrings in his ears they can't remember.
Yet one of them knows where to make a moon in each dark eye,
and then the real moon behind him
above a skyline bowered in red and yellow garlands,
maybe marigolds, geraniums, chrysanthemums
and roses— city flowers.
Why not put it on canvas? I call from the other world,
from a locked car, my window half-way up,
key in the ignition.
By the hissing, by the first flaring of their igniting cans,
I can see how the boys grant me the dignity of their contempt,
the tracks between us, however shattered,
still begging a deliverance,
littered as they are with home-made bongs
and free base lids, rolling papers, bent syringes.
They'd grant us all, in fact, our own colliding destinies
for what they're worth, for all they mean,
for what they will and won't reveal beyond this April morning—
now another difficult birthing, snow in the streets,
and a childhood blow by blow.
Now the prayer that on another day
seemed actually to bring the lost one home
like a fist through the door by the only light of earth.
Now the hammer smashing window after window.
And when the boys are done, they stop, no dates.
Just a looping line they say was his best rap,
and light a cigarette, one for the next.
At last they sign the dead one's tag for him
and then, below, their own:
Chek, Alert, Sparo, Abuze, Atone—
each name a tomb in which the spirit rots,
transmigrates, disappears, but not
before their cans explode like pistol shots, rain fire.

9

My Amaryllis

So this is the day the fat boy learns to take the jokes
by donning funny hats, my Amaryllis,
my buffoon of a flower,
your four white bullhorn blossoms like the sirens
in a stadium through which the dictator announces he's in love.
Then he sends out across the land a proclamation—
there must be music, there must be stays of execution
for the already dying.
That's how your pulpy sex undoes me and your seven
leaves unsheathed. How you diminish
my winter windows, and beyond them, the Atlantic.
How you turn my greed ridiculous.
Now it's as if I could believe in having children after forty,
or walking these icy streets, greet sullen strangers
like a host of former selves, so ask them in, of course,
and listen like one forgiven to their crimes.
Dance with us and all our secrets,
dance with us until our lies,
like death squads sent to an empty house, put down,
finally, their weapons, peruse the family
portraits, admire genuinely the bride.
Stay with me in this my exile
or my returning, as if to fuck the tyrant one more time.
O my lily, my executioner, a little stooped, here,
listing, you are the future bending
to kiss the present like a sleeping child.

Rune for the Parable of Despair

Little left of me that year— I had a vision
I was strata, atmosphere.
Or it was that the host entire coded in my blood
found voice and shrieked, for instance,
at what we now call *roads*
and I must maneuver freeways, bridges with these inside me
falling to their knees beating the ground howling.
One might well ask why they'd come forward—
fugitives flushed from a burning house,
converts fed down the aisles,
bumping and blubbering their way into revival light,
light so eroding, the human face is abberation,
the upright stance a freak
with no means otherwise.

Some things won't translate backwards.
Some things can't be undone,
though it takes years to learn this, years.
Such were the serial exhaustions of my beliefs,
whatever drug worn off that must belong to youth,
or to the feminine, or simply to the genes begun a wintering.
Then I knew the purest bitterness,
as if my heart were a wrecking ball,
my love for the man an iron bell used of the wind,
calling to task a population,
calling them in, as from these fields,
before the stone wheel became speech,
before fire dropped from the sky to be caged and carried into
        the caves.
And so they came to be with me,

whom I suspect was nothing more to them than shelter,
a ransomed hall, a shipwreck among dead trees,
the fallen branches lichen-studded,
which they dragged into my rooms.
And when the lights burned out they wept,

and when the heat was gone they gathered my rugs around them.
I'd never known how quickly a house
can be taken back, taken down,
nor will I grant myself the balm—
though it's been centuries—
that I was "blessed" to see it turned inside out,
the furniture thrown through the windows, and the books
to lie face up, riffling, swelling, until the pages
emptied into a thousand seasons,

books that once possessed the magnet pull of stars!
In the end I let them keep the house
the way they wanted, wash from the toilet,
hang yew boughs from the eaves,
my sturdy doors fallen from the hinges,
even my hair commingling with theirs—
huge animal clumps a-swirl in the eddies
of spiders' eggs and broken teeth and cemetery moss and pine needles—
until not one ornament was left that said I lived,
not even a drinking glass
I might have toasted with just as the clouds
shifted, my shadow disappeared,
O, drink from once before my leaving, leaving.
With any luck, I sang, I'll be in hell by Christmas.

The Way Into Stone

I hate to think how long I must lie here
face down, kissing myself
into the stone, or into the wood
becoming stone buried in water.
I hate to think how long it's going to take
for my dream silos to empty,
wind inside the bright theaters,
all that I am translating into stone—
my love for the taste of semen and the smell of my hair—
I for whom waiting does not come easily.
Nothing in my experience will say
what terrors last, which wear smoother than sea glass,
which love, which bitterness survives the frieze.
I have no gift for this waiting.
And yet I would be stone.
I would be stone by Philistia's gates
regathered for another execution, stone
which the builders refused
become the headstone of the corner.
I would learn to wait
the better to be stone, the many fallen into one,
cycloptic, deaf to the bells sounding that the soul has birthed
the last of her three children.
What do I know?
I am loose matter, sense and approbation,
the spirits of a house with six doors
slamming, merely the imprint of the autumn
and the dragonfly.
But it seems to me, when called upon to sing,
a stone is something to be listened to.
And that the coming of its song
sees all the words in books blackening
against their origins,
and the meanings rushing backwards as light
climbing the eight octaves.
And the roaring ceases in the ears of the drowned

13

at a stone's first heralding,
and cell by cell, the prisoners
make love to themselves in the asylums.
Oh yes, a stone's a mockingbird.
And midway through its aria
most of the angels flee the earth holding their ears,
and the beloved weeds are envious, and the trees,
summer or winter are longing to be stone,
and the walls would crumble to be stone again,
and the lilacs give up their color to be stone.

Rough Music

This is how it's done.
The villagers surround the house,
beat pots and pans, beat shovels to drain spouts,
crowbars to shutters, rakes
raining rake tines on corrugated washtubs, or wire
whips, or pitchforks, or horseshoes.
At first they keep their distance
as if to wake you like blackbirds, though the birds
have long since fled, flown deep into the field.
And for a while you lie still, you stand it,
even smile up at your crimes
accompanying, each one, the sunrise stuttering across the ceiling
like the sounds within the sounds,
like lightning inside thrum-tink, woman-in-wood-shoes-fall-
down-wooden-stairs, like wrong-wrong inside rung-rung,
brick-smacking-brick housing ice-breaking-ice-
breaking-glass . . .
I mention this since this is what my dreams
are lately, rough music,
as if all the boys to women I have been, the muses, ghost-
girls and the shadows of the ancestors
circled my bed in their cheap accoutrements
and banged my silver spoons on iron skillets, moor
rock on moor rock, thrust yardsticks into the fans.
Though I wake and dress and try
to go about my day,
room to room to room they follow me.
By evening, believe me, I'd give back everything,
throw open my closets, pull out my drawers spilling my hoard
of dance cards, full for the afterlife,
but my ears are bleeding.
I'm trapped in the bell tower during wind,
or I'm the wind itself against the furious, unmetered,
anarchical applause of leaves late autumns
in the topmost branches.
Now the orchestra at once throws down its instruments.

15

The doors in the house of God tear off their hinges—
I'm the child's fist drumming its mother's back,
rock that hits the skull that silences the martyr,
or I'm the martyr's tongue cut out, fire inside fire,
clapper back to ore, ore into the mountain.
I'm gone, glad, empty, good
riddance, some shoulder to the sea, the likeness
of a wing, or the horizon, merely, that weird mirage, stone-
skipping moon, the night filled up with crows.
I clap my hands.
They scatter, scatter, fistful after
fistful of sand on water, desert for desert, far from here.

For the Lost Adolescent

Even before he left for good I heard things in the fire,
heard fundamental moaning,
wind like a shoulder splintering a door.
I'd say, *Come here,* but he was lost to me.
I'd say, *Beloved, bring more wood up from the yard.*
But he was lost to me,
locked inside his name, the name itself
too big a house, or simply wilderness I only glimpsed sometimes.
And true, those days, looking out of my own eyes
I felt some former host behind me,
some bedrock stare, antediluvian, unchanging.
And he was horrified to see me watching
something like birds in the fire,
not their song but a scratching among rubble.
Something like rain then surely rain
if I shut my eyes.
Another year, another child,
this might have been the subject—
always penultimate, some claim for the beautiful,
the conditions of the lie gone up with goodness, all the same,
log after log, fire after fire, praise beyond pretense
for so primitive a thing, that first warmth
ransomed, a captive
of our need amid the ruin of a modern city!
And if I never recognized his voice inside me,
who could know?
A mother learns a code of sounds not yet a voice
and feels her way inside that heat
and then there's the holding while the world heals
or does not heal.
Life's long with and without him
where children passing on their way to school
no longer walk into his body.
As for their laughter, it's like the laughter in a dream
to which the sleeper barely smiles.

17

The Little Book of Hand Shadows

You who began inside me,
see a tortoise, a stork, a wolf come out of my hand.

Stand behind me, your shadow eclipsing
my shadow.

Make the cock crow by opening and closing two fingers.
We can be anyone now.

We can be spirit, ships homing, ten brothers in heaven.
Can you feel the sweet wind of their wing beats?

Can you smell the damp forest
as the walls fill up?

They breathe with things.
Crook your right forefinger which forms a paw.

Remember a crab moves a little sideways.
Pick me up like you used to and whirl me around.

Mother Hubbard's dog's begging.
Your Dapple Grey appears to be running.

Our shadows spill shadows.
They pool, they molt.

They grow out of the dark, they grow
out of themselves.

They crowd the ark, they crowd the world with their finger-ears
and thorny toes and their broken beaks

and knuckled hearts,
their broken beaks and knuckled hearts.

Akhmatova

So it had to be—
she doused the muse in kerosine, set her afire,
burned down the house of poetry.

It was a common kitchen stove.

She may have taken comfort in the warmth.

As for the cries of agony,
they would hereafter ghost the margins,
howl on in each cyrillic character omitted by decree—
"Dear Stalin, I have seen your way . . ."
"Dear Master, my poems belong to you now, to the state . . ."

since women are the most dispensable to tyrants.
Children can serve so beautifully as ransom.
They learn, besides, to carry any flag.
And men will die into a tortured beauty,
their broken arms laid straight against their sides,
their privates, even by their enemies, napkin-covered.

But women? Women are nothing.
They create the beast to know the depth of their desire.

They are like sparrows,
the battered coming closest for the grain,
or the part in the song where the oboe
breaks your heart like time itself,
then sneers to laughing.

If poetry is fire, it can't be written in the fire,
but sometime after, written in ashes
along the frozen road
if it be written down at all.

Yes, one can kill the thing not yet language,
feel one's mouth fill up with stones.

Better we all let go of the lie
that art can save a life, except perhaps its maker's,
and even then, one might argue
this is deception,

a false sun to fix the years
toward the day that one might simply see one's child again.

Surely inside her a vast Caina, a crown fire.
Oh, the lovers have given what they can
only to remain men.

They would say, "Something's gone out of her
and nothing offered in its place."

After the boy is taken a third time back to prison,
she would admit there's little left.
Life is a wild undoing!—

And when the poem she once burned down, burned
to the ground in the other life, reconstitutes itself inside her,
it is like someone else's shadow cursing,
figures approaching on the road.

It is a stone tied to a rope hurled round and round,
and the whistling,
and the terror of the blow.

At worst, it's just a door, the one that closes on us now,
and this lamp through the window.

See, they sit apart— old mother, aging son.
Oh, much, too much is lost.

Still, they begin.

Too much is lost— twenty-one years!
In fact they'll never come to like each other.
She cannot find the child's face in the man's.

In-House Harvest

So they'd start over, breed animals
for medicine, by firelight perform rituals,
though the human babies died,
the decimal lodged between the gene codes
like a new Rosetta stone.
They might as well have used divining rods
to ferret water, read the blood stains on the aprons
as the future, sent their sons into the caves
to emerge blind or visionary,
so envious of birds they'd bring them down,
suck the marrow from the wishbones,
burn out the warbler's eyes
that it might sing more sweetly.
Extinction by extinction, they found their way.
For instance they could sleep
high above the earth, or riding across country,
the lights in the compartments, if they wanted, on.
And even those who waited
in terrariumed or Christmas decorated houses
somehow went with them,
as those who rode made love to themselves
and not themselves, to phantoms,
dreamed fast through cultivated fields,
through cities, where the dead, the nearly dead
and newly born were arranged
by sex, by need, behind many numbered doorways.
And in a room one could elect to enter
that moved up or down,
they would be visited by ghosts in green
wearing the masks, perhaps, of time—
green, they'd tell you.
Green was easy on the eyes.
As if you'd witnessed the arc of the stone tool
thrown through history,
delivered, shining, in the surgeon's hand,
he opened the body kept alive

for each spare part, a liver, lungs, and heart,
in a church of a place without music.
And the other wheeled in and opened, too,
you couldn't see its face,
nor could you say if it was old or young,
man or woman, who received the in-house harvest.
Nor was there singing afterwards
in the chancels of the round room, no one
to direct the host, nor did the surgeon labor
longer, the length and color of the thread the same
for donor and survivor.
It was a silence like translation, merely
the cadence of a story, ◡′ ◡′ ◡′
  ◡′, the one they longed to hear against the one
already known that told of a death so bright
it burned impressions on the rock of their species,
while the glass plates bearing the pictures of their wars
became the greenhouse windows.

Rock, Scissors, Paper

1

It ended when he popped one of the three of the order
coleoptera in his mouth. Two hands weren't enough for Darwin—
*He stares at a yellow flower for minutes at a time. His family
don't know what to do with him—.*
                                        The beetle bit his tongue, and
    like the dragon-
angel Michael, who spit out the fallen world's new genus
as he waded in an orchard through paradisiacal weeds,

Darwin spat by a tree and laughed, son of the theological classes.

Now think of the mind, said Freud, as the Eternal City
(as if *angel* could mean *messenger* or *coin*, and *phylum*,
tribe), think of the palaces of the Caesars on the Palatine
next to the temples of the gods. So many kingdoms

piling up— not one destroyed— residing whole, and every
sort of traffic there, the Tiber clogged. Our species

dreams across those rooftops. Why aren't we happy?—

2

like Marx's universal arming of the people, a species
crowed out imagining itself reborn above a rubble.

And yet the places, wrote Darwin, which most order
my thoughts are those, boundless, stratified as the nine legions
of angels, places without habitation, without trees, a kingdom

of food-gatherers, the fire-bearers upright before the herds.
See how they're moving toward the sea? Each lamp represents a family

along the lava beach. The nets they throw into the shallows
cannot contain their origins. They're happy here, *a class*

which has radical chains, which is the dissolution of all classes . . .

Freud: And do you remember how when we were young, we used, day
after day to walk Vienna's streets reciting psalms, as though the genus
of our race weren't something to be spat upon? And on Sundays
we'd go to the museums, peruse the fossils

3

in the long list of extinctions, Brother. Now here we are in Athens.
We have come a long way, as far as Babel from the new
    "linguistic phylum."

Europe's alive with talk. Outside the Prater
they're burning books, *The Talmud, The Origin of Species,*
and mine on jokes! What company! The fires
illuminate the ring of faces white with fear, fear's geniuses . . .

Rock smashes scissors, scissors cut paper,

paper covers rock, and the rest shall I set in order
when I come . . .
                No one knows the name of the ferryman
whom the good luck child advised, a precursor to the working classes.
I'm tired, he cried, of rowing. How do I get off this river?
When you reach the far shore, said the heir to the kingdom,
leap off! Hand your pole to your passenger.

Marx: In its earliest phases society took the form of the family,

4

the clan, the tribe. On what foundations are the present families
of the bourgeois based? On capital. On private gain.

When the gods changed two Athenian sisters into birds, Philomela
became a nightingale. But could she sing without her tongue?
And did she know her sister, the swallow, whose kingdom
is the evening? Who does not sing? *Cruelty arises*

from the instinct for mastery, a trait not peculiar to our species.

And even birds (Darwin) have vivid dreams, a left and a right
cerebral hemisphere. Their songs are learned and can be classified
by dialect. A northern and a southern sparrow trill
a slightly different series.
                  We have our orders,

sang the young officers who took Anna Freud away.

I knew then, dying or not, that we must leave—. The genes

hold the journey. At the base of the cranial vault, hunger, thirst,

5

wanting, what is called *fight or flight* ignite the pulse, the genie
in the lamp. *When we stood up, we lost our way.*

Near eighty, Anna Freud (deceased) narrates home movies of **the family**
in which she is a girl bringing her father flowers she's picked,
she says, from her cousin's country gardens. *The orders*

came that spring. The women there— they are my father's sisters— **died**
in the camps, the ones waving, see? And the children beside them.
                                                    Phylloid,

their names on the tree diagrammed in the museum, set under
        glass,
protected from the million fingerprints, each thumb's swirl
        classified
at birth, black at the center, at the crow-eye of the funnel.

As children we made faces on our fists, some cross-species,
two blind eyes below the knuckle along the metacarpal index,
the thumb an awful mouth, an old man's, a tortoise's, saying:
        Then shall the kingdom
be likened unto a vineyard. Or heaven's a wedding.

6

It's exactly like a tree, Heaven's a door. The kingdom
is like a man traveling in a far country, *as if to make a marketable*
value out of virtue, love, etc. Heaven's congenital . . .

In fact, the hand-man sang, I want to marry a lighthouse keeper
and live by the side of the sea . . . as though he were a specialist
of dreams, god of the big and the little shipwrecks,

his mouth torn open, half-dead, half-grinning, whispering tne family

names, generation by generation, each keeper of the flame
listed on brass plaques greening on any lighthouse, an extinct class.

And the robot beam clicks on clicks off above you
or the fog horn blasts the chlorophyll
air, blasts through you, merely matter, scissors-cut-paper,

who cannot fall out of this world. And if I cannot order
for myself (Freud) this 'oceanic feeling,' there's not a little

7

that is ancient still buried in the soil of the ordained
city. *Here is the church, here is the steeple,* here,

the cave whose rock swellings form the animal's haunches. The
    kingdom's
indivisible where the artist lay his hand under the herds
and through a blow-pipe spit his signature, even the phyllode
moons in his fingernails erased by pigments

made from pollen, dirt, flower petals, blood, the colors fired and
    classified

on a wheel like a cornea, blind to itself.
                                On the other side
we'll know the shaman by his blackened hand, as here, his genius
cannot fill the five fingered emptiness. By my life, listen,

(Marx) I would create your own, and your families',
who will inherit nothing but these fields. I would be mediator,

lightning rod, dream and/or destiny machine between you. And
    the species
and you will know me as a part of your own nature . . .

E N V O Y :   those first cold mornings our father blew into our hands
to warm them   and in the afternoons after our classes
we were mad to be outside   we'd bury one another in the leaves
we did not think *those who have gone before us*
the kingdom's progenitors   not *the only species*
we just lay down and closed our eyes as beech by oak
by sycamore the leaf-light disappeared and we stayed still a while
families at the gravesites   or leapt up shouting
look and look at me   *but who will take my hand first in the long*
receiving line   watch me I'd call   *we have our orders*
and sometimes they answered look at you   watch me I'd call
from a branch above the biggest pile of leaves   watch me
and then I dove and I could barely hear them
calling *good-luck-to-yous   good-luck   good-luck   good-luck*

Morning After A Blizzard

What could they possibly need to bury in heaven?
Imaginary playmates, secret lives
who wait their turn,
perhaps relieved to be going among their kind,
among the mortal necessities,
the wheelchairs, trusses, heaps of bifocals,
the huge corrective shoes,
until those foyers at the entrance resemble stations
in one of history's recurring dreams.
Some nights one hears a train approaching.
Who'll be assigned to dig the graves
in which each figure of despair lies down now in obscurity
so like these snowbanks, pine-splayed without
relief, pine-dappled here?
Even the shovel is transcription, a dream toy,
unless it scrape the earth.
My mother says her death will defy gravity,
her body beyond its shadow rinsed of memory,
so white it seals the eyes, and all they've seen,
the rooms buried in which we sat,
a family always wrong year after year,
snowfall by snowfall,
the mother weeping, the father praying aloud,
each word out of his mouth
another cave furnished by shipwreck,
the children silent,
the daughters still in their nightgowns
dozing against each other or lost in the analogy,
lost, as part way through a wish that feels like distance,
Roman light, or sea glass, glint off the Atlantic
glimpsed from the air.
What could be monument toward this lightness?
Faith turned to stone?
This is what it was to be alive, saved.
This was love as we knew it.

The Story of the Lighthouse

The autumn sun was such riding the ocean
the white brick lighthouse branded our eyes.

Blinking, we saw *lighthouse, lighthouse*.

Earlier, walking to meet my friend for breakfast,
I passed through couples
emerging from their rooms,
the women groomed and lovely,
the distance between sexes intact entirely.

Or let me put it this way.

In the motel windows their reflections eclipsed my own.
If I was happy to be lost and free,
the unmade beds, like boats loose from their moorings,
seemed to drift out toward me.

I might have called that ocean gilt,
though it refuses reductions.
As for the sky above the water, it swallows language,
the way wind can carry off a voice.

The lighthouse bore a plaque of all its keepers.

I wanted to take my best friend's hand
as though we are not born of our mothers
who are the fire on a horizon,
starboard a round room, its scaffolds narrowing,
who carry in them, as we will all our lives,
ova anonymous as the earth
beneath headstones of sailors lost at sea.

Beneath one's feet, not even bones!

It's like a ringing in the ears.

Not born of the mothers,
but of the dark called to,
a faint arterial vectoring shot through with static,
the one chance pressed close, breathed in.

Say this is where we've come from, broken against stone,
drifting like dresses on the waves at first light
beyond the rocks that catalog the elegies
someone must keep repainting—
rocks risen today above a calm sea.

You can make out the names of the wrecks downed here,
The Laura Barnes, The Annie C. McGuire,
ships named for women.

FOR S. M.

Spring

I can't find your hair among my clothes
nor will the birds this spring
where you loved to groom yourself
in the sunlight,
the mirror hung from a branch,
your shadow lengthening
as if to reach beyond me as always,
reach across time beyond this ending like furniture
shipwrecked in a field,
the caravan moved on,
the owners and their whereabouts unknown,
even the child lost who was birthed under the sky
far down the light,
lost among the pine groves like strong men to lean on.
Never again will I pillage lilacs
just to shake dew on your face,
behead the roses,
and pressing two petals to my lips,
kiss into you the taste of roses.
My shadow lies down with the memory of your shadow
in this house without a roof,
this room whose floor is grass,
this last year's nest ransacked for what of you
I might find here before the thickets close,
a wild green swallows everything.
I'll never love as I loved you against my disappearing.

Five Smooth Stones

The man who wants no children
is like five smooth stones.
His is the face that haunts the orphans,
proctors their dreams.
In the waking hours they wonder
who it is such sympathy arrives in.
So he is used this way.
He's given birth to something.
The man who wants no children dreams of children.
He would give his clothes away,
his overcoat and boots.
He walks the streets opening gates for the yard dogs
and the vagrants who live in boxes.
He washes with them in the public fountains,
and when he is alone he thinks of them,
and at the founding of the great museums.
He is beloved of his landlord.
Who wants no children loves women
who forget to lock their doors
while the weeds destroy the garden.
He is lucky.
There are many such women fat with faith,
fat with atavistic ritual beliefs,
beautiful women who smell of talc, semen, lilacs.
He has loved.our children after all,
has on his shoulders carried little ones
across tide pools
as if each child were the world's store,
or a lamp and he the fire bearer.
Oh yes, he is a lighthouse.
He protects his seed, or spills it in secret
by the wayside.
Call him both brilliant, then, and lucky.
When he dies he dies with his heart intact,
and his soul becomes a cloud whose shadow
dissipates above the desert.

For the first stone is the lode stone
and the second is his headstone, and the third
one parts the waters,
and the fourth is buried with him,
and the fifth is never found.
The man who wants no children
is like five smooth stones.

Chekhov's Darling

Then came the day even the water glass felt heavy
and I knew, as I'd suspected, I grew lighter.
I grew lighter, yes.
Say, have you ever fainted?
Such a distinct horizon as you are raised
above your pain—
And after forty years they entered Canaan . . .
Don't tell me about turning from what might change you,
taking the second, not the first compartment
in the revolving door,
tossing the note in the bottle back into the channel.
No, the afternoon was not a practice for another.
The birds, they flew.
The virus spread throughout the city.
It was a real day, and I grew lighter.
And I asked my friend if I could hold his arm
to keep myself from rising.
I picked up the rare city stones and put them in my pocket.
Still, I could see how the buildings dreamed themselves
backwards to rubble, and the sun-smashed
windows, the mortar back to sand.
I watched Orpheus in the flesh set broken china
into the fissures of the sidewalk after he'd poured the grout
and smoothed it with his trowel.
Then, blue shard by blue shard he made a sky of the abyssal
sepulchers across which the homeless
floated, much as I, where
the trains passed, and the ground shook.
It was like standing inside singing, knowing something of its need.
It was the troubled child grown old, happy, the lost in sight
of home, and born for this.
There is a sadness older than its texts
that will outlive the language,

like the lover who takes you by the roots of your hair.
In this way I was awake, I was light,
I grew lighter,
though I had not yet been lifted.

Apples

Everyone brings flowers
and I bring apples sent from Milton,
Josephus, Hesperides, three
red, one golden, like a flower.

It is the evening of his eleventh labor,
the prophets gathering at his bedside.

Everyone brings flowers but I bring apples,
place one in his palm
and close his fingers around the seasons
like faces, ballast,

three red, one golden.
Who knows which he'll recognize,

what phantom feature, son
or daughter calling
past dark from the orchard trees.

I bring down apples burning, burning yellow
in the white room.

Even the window is nothing to these three
red, one golden, like a fire
we warm our hands over,

our hands over his hands
in this small camp above the city, everyone
with flowers.
I have brought apples,
three red, one golden, like a flower.

Gypsy Moths

Lord in the late lap of summer, these sepulchers in the trees—
how did I miss such blatant countermotion,
the larvae inching upwards
to free-fall and weave above my road
this spectral trapeze, filament by filament?
Thus scaffolded, the nurseries and birthing chambers.
Now occupied in topmost outer branches
these tents lashed down to leaf-spine, leaves.
A wild string game!—
lanterns hung through-out the woods,
each holding the daylight a little past sunset.
Not for the first time do I understand
that one might live a whole life and die
never having learned the worst about one's self,
this knowledge the one dry room above the torrents,
a bottle with a note inside traversing oceans—
a bathysphere whose climate doesn't change,
though the message expires,
the seasons shift outside it, and the weather
as the continents, torn apart, they drift.
Dismantled, the metaphor reveals what's wrong
inside the thing— bad air, discoloration.
Then one must learn how not to hate it,
how not to hate one's own need—
love the father in the child, for instance,
though the man himself's a tyrant,
or love the tyrant though he hates his seed.
I too have worshipped the wrong gods
so that my enemies became my judges.
They led my secrets
away from me and paraded them through the streets,
each wearing the costume she had chosen, believe me,
out of misreading of the occasion.
But who in the world could have prepared them,
made to dance in their dressy shoes
across rotting earth and broken bottles,

41

some leading with their left,
some simply graceless, limping to the drum beat,
the raucous mock-falsettos.
Even the child spinning, tripping on her robe
like the robes of the Greek chorus.
It was useless to call out that I had wanted her.
Perhaps the mob would riot, and be right to.
Even at her conception I was cynical,
too world-wise to believe
that, brought to term and birthed,
her significance could change me.
I call the child a "she".
My own sentimental coloring of what I recklessly threw away
(for fear— imagine— of losing the love of the father)
and sat up on the table.
What could it matter these years later
whether I hate the fact of myself
legs wide in the dead middle of the act,
or mourn the loss, or both?
By the world's rules, neither.
Simply, I went against my nature,
no less sacred than another's,
as if time could be lyrical
but I possessed the vision of the mole the cat drops at my feet,
never to catch up with or run back toward myself.

Forty-two Years of Dreams

It happens I have let loose this morning
forty-two years of dreams,
let loose like your harvests of leaves every autumn
my thousands, my crowds—
the stand-ins, lovers,
the lies like animal shadows,
or the child disappeared and looked for
all one's life—
that they might meet someday in the world saying,
"You were the one made to stand in the corner—
Take my seat all the way to Manhattan,"
or, "You who lived in the cellar, welcome!
See how the light becomes you?"
This summer's flowers are ground to cinders,
and their shadows are lost that cast them,
like a net, into time.
They were things and took their place
as long as the body lived.
So I lean into an idea of your arms.
I look up through the pine and my face stays dry,
though it's raining.
Here the clouds are great churches.
From their ledges the worst of intentions peer down,
and the best, my broken-hearted.
Let them jump now jump it is written,
knowing nothing, at last, will save them
who cannot believe their death, even as they fall.
And I am the dream with a pin in his hip,
his bride in streetclothes watching
this doomed trapeze under a sky bower,
like those pitched over graves for a time
until the sod's laid down
over a door, light into the earth.

London Zoo

Love takes liberties, so much gets by us,
as if the trick were learning
not to want what doesn't want us.
Here, for instance, the animals seem happy.
Even the sparrows stay.
Children stop to feed them
on the paths between the cages.
A bird dives underwater,
stripes on the zebra and the zebra fish.
What we want what we want is a lyric for forgetting,
like the skill to fall backwards
through the genes past wanting,
past fear of falling, "faith,"
as if the tombs of the muses were so many
bombed out houses the homeless
set up camp inside,
careful to turn their backs at night on those roofless rooms,
careful to keep their fires going
where the little rain-soaked wall paper flowers shine
by the moon-dogged moon *blessings on the hunter*,
and on the wanderer, his keep-sake soul,
though the list of his extinctions approach
his numbered wishes, though his child be a moon-calf,
though he spit on the angel
whose likeness is a hanged man cut down some midnight
four centuries ago, and then by torch-light,
opened in the alley, the hands severed
and set aside on which the pale hairs stand
as in love, or terror of ascent,
the dead-bright blood caught in a bowl of sand
and, free-based, distills the pigment
for the background's first spring or autumn cypresses.

A Thousand Eclipses

What a day to come back to the world—
dry-mouthed and groggy from the medication,
my lover's semen leaking from me,
I lie down under a tree
whose pin-hole leaves become a camera lucida
freeing a surf of whole notes
mackerel scaled,
east light and to the east
wind driven across the hilltop campus.
The ground drowns in eclipses, loosed scores, nets full,
some ancient haul I could be part of
because I've stopped struggling against my sadness,
some ancient thing remembering me—
love, or pain
contained inside the octave,
only the octave,
that run of thirteen counting the minor keys,
even as the asylum bars become the staves
on which a new music hangs itself.
And oh, what a weird light
by which to find, at last, faith's limits!—
never to suffer more
or less than my blood allows
with its fixed spells and transmigrations.
How many times I've taken an axe to the silence!
Have heard in my bad ear forests felled,
as if I could bring back with me
a death from another time
and not be broken by the weight,
recreant of the joys
that hold me here between the strata.
I come to worship what I mistake
and misremember, what I think I see
that's neither blade nor blow nor vessel fragments flying.
Of my many selves I know them best who cannot speak,

for whom these early autumn shadows
are unliftable, unliftable,
for whom, just as I rise,
the crickets cease
and the old scars across my wrist
ache like the static from the other world
as the season cools.
Ten moons whiten in my fingernails.

My Phantom Escort, the Milkweed

My phantom escort, the milkweed,
blown across the asphalt—
that hopeless, but of itself undaunted—
said there was some way, some possibility
in loving you against history,
who ushered me doorway by doorway
inside my skin inside another hotel room.
There we were nothing blessed with
and without honor, liars
as we came. No one we'd want to know
might understand all too well
how afterward we weren't changed,
even dressed, and on the street again, original.
We'd ride a few blocks together in a taxi.

Blue Willow

The park had been plowed under,
the soccer and the cricket fields,
the gazebo dismantled.
Far left, in what were once the gardens,
all the dedicated benches with their little metal plaques—
to my husband John who loved these roses . . .
faced the excavations like galleries
set up before an execution.
It was the perfect end to a troubled year.
They'd held each other only after nightmares.
And once let in their flat, against advice,
they'd fallen into bed to wake at sunset,
jet-lagged, still exhausted, the view
torn up, black soil.
But something flashed in the furrows
and flashed again a little farther out.
In the last of the daylight
she dressed and climbed the fence,
touched down backwards
and as her good shoes filled with mud
she saw the sky in the china and the glass,
acre on acre, like a dream ceiling
shattered among the tree roots,
spilled up onto the paths.
She picked her way half way across the field
filling her pockets,
then turned to wave to him.
Bring bags! she called. *Just bring them to the fence!*
But he climbed over too.
By evening they'd collected hundreds,
soaked in the tub clay pipe bowls and porcelain
dresser knobs, too much black glass,
and his favorites, the white
marble fragments, as from an urn.
The best of the china
bore no insignia,

though they thought they recognized some Wedgewood,
Spode's Blue Willow,
a crescent portrait of those famous
gardens floating up from the pitch silt—
buoyed beneath the surface the bamboo bridge,
the pagoda in the distance.
The next morning they went out again,
this time with baskets.
The neighbors stood on their balconies
and watched, or put on boots
and joined them.
From the asphalt path a man
pushing his wife in a wheelchair shouted.
She'd found a pottery platter lip
bordered by butterflies.
She gave it to them later when they lay their finds
on the benches, when her husband
recalled the bombings.
See there, he gestured with a muddy shard,
they's all replaced—.
They looked across the park to their windows.

Christmas Rain

Here is the tree
whose topmost branches will not again green.
This evening the crows gather
merely to watch a sparrow

with a bit of Christmas rain in its beak fly
into the hard pine.

Now over the backyards
of the rich, sparrow attacks crow—
chases it down toward its own miserable death,
the nest, of course, abandoned.

Now the crows fly as one,
perhaps toward the ocean trees.

Well, it's justice this year to live without hope.

Nothing made of fear alone can last
like nothing made exclusively of happiness.

Nursing the Hamster

And it was true.
A death so slight they could hold it in their palms
opened up rooms inside them
according to their need,
his like a closet.
He'd kick the doors out daily.
Hers was a wilderness
through which she'd wander calling his name.
After that, believe me,
nothing went right for them.
Say what you like.
Say even grief seeks some proportion.
For death to count at all,
that which goes in the earth beneath the yew must weigh
the sum of its displacement.
Or say the animal was mostly metaphor,
an abberation born in a cage
to live three years, far from its kind.
And was it ever, anyway, entirely itself, even to the boy?
"It's like a cat," he'd say,
or "like a tiny puppy . . .
It's like a bird that cannot fly away."
Still, they had fed it the medicine through an eye-dropper,
its silly wheel gone silent.
And the boy lay down and put it on his chest.
He let it sleep there through the evenings.
So they had hope
the night before it died,
the way suddenly it nested, its pouches packed
so full, the thing was laughable,
barely maneuvering the bright plastic maze,
stopping here and there to rest, panting, plowing on.
Who can say which sadness when takes over,
becomes rudder?
Who can name for another what moors, what charts the drift?
Yes, they had laughed and laughed,

the way laughter
buoys faith, bullies the truth back into hiding.
And the animal, without analogy,
the animal in some last instinct which merely parallels desire,
wanted it all, wanted more, which is to be alive.

Notes

Page 6: "Late Summer;" Therese de Lisieux (1873–97) died in a convent, along with her sisters, of tuberculosis. She was affectionately called, "The Little Flower of Jesus," and she saw it as one of her missions to bury dead animals she found in the woods, or along roads.

The poem is a response to an article I read that reported the story of a mother who had assisted her son with AIDS to commit suicide.

Page 8: "Tombs of the Muses" takes its title from a phrase in Emerson's essay, "The Poet," in which he describes language as "fossil poetry . . . the tombs of the muses." There is reference to *tags* in the poem; tags are the secret names of individuals in street gangs, and sometimes the names of the gangs themselves, and with which they sign their wall art. If one's tag is identified or stolen, one takes a new tag, the point being to keep one's true identity a secret.

Page 15: "Rough Music" was an ancient and medieval practice in Friesland, parts of Holland, and later the Fen Country in England, among other places. When members of a community became aware of a thief, an adulterer, or a murderer living among them, they would gather outside the house of the condemned and bang pots and pans, sticks, tools, anything that would make a racket, until the condemned was driven out of his or her house by the noise, driven from the community never—as was the common law—to return.

Page 19: "Akhmatova" touches on a story about the Russian poet whose son Lev was imprisoned three times by Stalin because of his mother's refusal to stop writing personal lyrics, or to write poems for the State. In the Politburo's official condemnation of her work, she is described as "a nun or a whore combining harlotry with prayer."

At Lev's third arrest Anna Akhmatova did try to appeal to Stalin and she wrote some terrible poems in praise of him. At this time she also burned "Requiem." Many years later, after Stalin's death, the entire poem came back to her and she wrote it down again. Lev was not released from prison until the fifties. Biographers write that after Lev's release mother and son had a turbulent relationship.

Page 22: "In-House Harvest" takes its title from a medical term: when organ donor and recipient happen to be in the same hospital at the same time, this coincidence is called an in-house harvest.

The end of this poem is written from a collision of two stories, the first one reported after the bombing of Hiroshima and Nagasaki. The flashes of light at the time of the bombs' impacts were so bright that they burned impressions of the dead onto stone.

The second story concerns Matthew Brady, the Civil War photographer. When the war was over, Brady went bankrupt, the public no longer wanting to view and/or remember the war. Because his photographs were impressed on glass panes, he began selling off those panes in order to pay his debtors. The biggest buyers were greenhouse owners who used the plates for windows. Erased by sunlight, many of Brady's negatives simply disappeared.

Page 24: "Rock, Scissors, Paper" is a sprung sestina. Because the taxonomy scale has seven end-words instead of six, I decided to make each stanza fourteen lines, using the end-words every other line. As a result, a strange thing happened: the end-word "class" and variations always ended up as the fourth word repeated in each stanza, like the hub of a wheel.

The game "rock, scissors, paper" is said to be one of the oldest and most international of children's games, perhaps because it is non-verbal, more like sign than spoken language.

At least half of "Rock, Scissors, Paper," maybe more, is made up of quotes from many different sources, among them Darwin's *Voyage of the Beagle*, Marx's *Communist Manifesto*, Freud's *Civilization and Its Discontents*, and letters to his brother, film clips of Anna Freud narrating home movies (which can be viewed in the Freud house in Hampstead, London), the new testament, myth, the lyrics of children's games, and songs popular at the turn of the century. To trace them all here would be pedantic and silly and would rob what I hope to be the effect of a fugue, or Greek chorus, or a relay race, one voice handing off to another.

Page 48: "Blue Willow" is a china pattern designed by Spode in England in the late 1600's. It has been copied by many manufacturers of china—a deep blue and white drawing of an exotic garden containing, among other blooming foliage, cherry trees and willows. The white space that is water inlets around several pagodas. Over a bridge march three men, one said to be an angry father. In the sky above the garden are two birds in flight, each facing the other.

The story goes that the birds are human lovers who, as they fled the wrath of the angry father, were turned into birds by benevolent gods.

The setting for this poem is Paddington Park in Maida Vale, London, originally a seventeenth century dump, and later badly bombed during the Blitz. In 1989 the park was torn up to be redesigned and refurbished, and, as the excavations began, much old china, bottles and marble fragments, along with window panes and debris from the bombings were turned up in the soil. At that time I was living on the park with my husband and son and we collected much china and glass which we brought home with us.

A NOTE ABOUT THE AUTHOR

DEBORAH DIGGES was raised in Jefferson City, Missouri. She is the author of two earlier books of poems, *Vesper Sparrows* (1986) and *Late in the Millennium* (1989), the first of which received the Delmore Schwartz Memorial Poetry Award from New York University. She has received grants for her writing from the Ingram Merrill Foundation, the Guggenheim Foundation and the National Endowment for the Arts. Her memoir, *Fugitive Spring*, was published in 1992. She has taught in the graduate writing divisions of New York, Boston, and Columbia universities. She is Associate Professor of English at Tufts University and lives in Amherst, Massachusetts.

A NOTE ABOUT THE TYPE

This book is set in Linotype Electra, a typeface designed by W. A. Dwiggins (1880–1956), one of the most distinguished type and book designers of the twentieth century. It is a typeface of great originality and distinction in that it does not depend on historical models. Dwiggins as book designer produced outstanding work for a number of publishers, but his collaboration with Alfred A. Knopf, lasting for several decades, is incomparable.

Composition by Heritage Printers, Inc., Charlotte, North Carolina
Printed and bound by Quebecor Printing, Kingsport, Tennessee